HOME
IN THE
DARK

HOME
IN THE
DARK

Poems
by
Jay Udall

*To Miriam Sagan,
with warm regards*

SUNSTONE
PRESS

SANTA FE

Sunstone books may be purchased for educational, business,
or sales promotional use. For information please write:
Special Markets Department, Sunstone Press, P.O. Box 2321,
Santa Fe, New Mexico 87504-2321.

Library of Congress Cataloging-in-Publication Data:

Udall, Jay, 1959–
     Home in the dark : poems / by Jay Udall.
          p. cm.
     ISBN: 0-86534-355-1
     I. Title.

PS3621.D35 H66 2002
811'.6—dc21   2002070616

SUNSTONE PRESS
Post Office Box 2321
Santa Fe, NM 87504-2321 / USA
(505) 988-4418 / orders only (800) 243-5644
FAX (505) 988-1025
www.sunstonepress.com

Published in

For Suzanne and Rachel,

the women beyond my dreams

Acknowledgments

The following poems first appeared in these publications:

"The Green Leaf" in *Manzanita Quarterly*

"Dreamer" in *The Mid-America Poetry Review*

"How the World Dreams Us" in *The Alliance*

"Message to Descartes" in *Talking River Review*

"First Identity" in *The Eastern Oregonian*

"First Sky" in *Bryant Literary Review*

"The Tilelayer" in *Thin Air*

"In the Check-Out Line" in *Out of Line*

"Santa Fe River, West of St. Francis" in *The Lucid Stone*

"A Boy Fishing" in *Potato Eyes*

"Long Distance" in *Connections: An Anthology of Poems on Friendship*

"A Far Country" in *Potpourri*

"How to Change" and "Arrival" in *Baybury Review*

"Walking the Silence" in *The Oregonian*

"The Old Woman and the Gray Cat" in *Switched-on Gutenberg*

"Letter of Apology to the Nonliving" in *Comstock Review*

"Crossing Space" in *The Concho River Review*

"Gathering Stones" in *Sin Fronteras*

"Crawdad," "Blood Ties," "Ambition," "Kochia," "Unidentified," "The Transient River," "Tracking," "Home in the Dark," and "The Time of Great Blue Heron" in the chapbook *First Identity* (Redgreene Press, 2001)

Contents

II

A Far Country / 51

III

Home in the Dark / 81

Preface

When Jim Smith, the publisher of Sunstone Press, first suggested that I write a preface for this volume of poems, I balked at the idea. I began writing poetry as a refugee from academia, having successfully escaped the life of a summa cum laude literature scholar. I was an excellent interpreter of other people's writing, but felt deeply dissatisfied, and then I realized why: I wanted to create my own literature. With absolutely no formal training in the process, I wrote my first poems by intuition, giving myself the freedom to write whatever came to me, teaching myself as I went. Within five years my work had appeared in a good number of magazines, and Bellowing Ark Press had published my first book of poetry, *Learning the Language*.

I continued to write by feel, rather than by rules or prevailing fashion, developing over time an almost superstitious fear that too much explanation and analysis (note the long shadow of academia) would make the magic vanish as quickly as it had come. So when Jim mentioned an author preface, I froze dead in my tracks. "Evoke, don't explain!" I've always admonished my students. If I followed Jim's suggestion, I might end up violating my own first principle—and much worse.

Jim's good sense and gentle insistence won out in the end, of course. Yet I still believe that my fear was—and is—not wholly unfounded, at least in one sense. Our formal education encourages us to look at a poem primarily as a *thing*, an object, a re-creation of experience that contains an idea or meaning. This is an excellent way to kill poetry. It's vastly more interesting and useful to approach a poem as an *event*, a happening in language, because this is closer to how serious poetry is actually written—and closer to the kind of experience it seeks to initiate. A good poem draws us into a relationship of imagination, intuition, intellect, memory, emotion, breath and pulse, an experience that is wonderfully idiosyncratic to each reader, and even different for the same reader on different occasions. Above all, this is what I wish for the reader of these poems.

It was not my conscious intention while writing these poems, but in hindsight I see in them an effort to explore a fundamental paradox. On the one hand, each of us is a unique individual with a unique awareness; no one experiences the exact same thing at the exact same time in the exact same way. On the other hand, as the life sciences, the Native Americans, and the mystics of the world's wisdom traditions continue to tell us, we are more deeply implicated in the whole of life than we dare to imagine.

These seemingly irreconcilable perspectives are the two poles between which many of the poems seem to gravitate; sometimes both are at work in a single poem.

A poem can begin anywhere, with the smallest object or image—a wildflower, a weed, a face, a scrap of memory—yet it should move into unexpected terrain. I want my poems to be grounded in the details of daily experience, in the physical world, in what is close at hand, but also to touch otherness, strangeness, mystery. This is what I look for, what I pursue, in the writing—a sense of surprise, of stumbling onto something unforeseen.

To work with the unfolding of a poem entails risk. I must be willing to follow where it leads, even when it asks me to enter some new wilderness of perception and experience. In other words, I must be willing to change. Poetry, if pursued in depth, is subversive and restorative. It delves beneath custom and convention, beneath all forms of received wisdom, beneath all fixed theories and interpretations, returning us to a sense of life as we know it to be in our deeper moments: beautiful, terrible, paradoxical. Writing poetry is, for me, a way of staying alive.

These poems represent hundred and hundreds of hours of hard, pleasurable work—the best kind of work I know. In the end, though, they feel like gifts. I offer them to the reader in the same spirit.

I

How the World
Dreams Us

The Green Leaf

                    of a burning
                              bush
                        burning

in the night
while I sleep

keeps singing
          singing
        its other

names: sunlight dirt carbon time
oxygen cellulose chlorophyll rain
that once kissed these lips

and will again
          singing
        singing

blood and fiber of my mother
and my father, this hand, sustenance
of the yet unborn:
                    alligators
kittens crickets grasses
grizzlies hawks ospreys kids
a green leaf
                this form
                        being
                dreamed
keeps
    singing
being.

Dreamer

As a boy I'd catch you slipping away
in scattered moments, gazing off
at nothing, eyes fixed on some invisible
distance, as you sat in a chair
at the kitchen table, or stood
at a window, and once with your razor
raised halfway to your half-foamed chin,
water dripping off your hand,
your body so still, as if emptied
of yourself, yourself emptied
into the place of your seeing.

You were always leaving
in other ways, too.
Your back was a door closing, shut
tight, no knob for my small hands.

A familiar voice is speaking
and the sound of a question
hooks me, drawing me back.
What did you say? I ask.

Crawdad

Ten years old and seeking
my brown plastic crawdad bucket
in early summer, freed from school, time
come round again for hunting the living treasures
that hid in certain streams under certain rocks
and sand that swirled up in the water like smoke
while I looked through, concentrating on the place
a rock had been, the water slowly clearing, clearing
until I could see all the way down there: crawdad
or no crawdad, all that mattered in the world.

Spying the lip of my bucket beneath
the laundry table, hidden like a secret
back there, behind dusty old boxes.
Crouching down, reaching in, feeling
for the handle, grabbing, pulling
the unexpected weight knocking
against the boxes, cold liquid
splashing on my forearm, fingers
releasing the bucket falling
rightside up: cloudy brown water
swirling with glittery bits of mica.

Pouring the bucket in the green weeds
and dead leaves at yard's edge, far above
the river flowing through the billowing trees
in the distance below. Wet rocks and sand
from last summer, and then—now
here he *was*, climbing up on a rock
the same green-brown color, like a rock
come to life, green-brown shell and claws
gleaming wet in the sunlight, feelers
feeling the change, the rewarming air.

How had he survived so long long long
alone where I had left him, the biggest one
ever, the prize, saved as proof, then forgotten
in his dark corner of the laundry room, unseen
and unknown—that blind life living on and on
below the onflowing days.

Grabbing him back of his claws, between
thumb and forefinger so he couldn't pinch,
placing him in the river, claws spread
out like wings in the green water,
riding the surface a moment, then
                    sinking,
                    sinking
out of sight,
            carried off
                    by the current,
hidden deep again
in the body of the world,
where he couldn't tell
what he knew,
how he rose
from the dark
and found me.

Chemistry Set

A metal box of magic your mother gave you
for those kind hours or entire days when your leukemia
would seem to forget itself and fall back to sleep.
If we could find just the right combination
of compounds, we would make a wondrous thing:
an explosion—a burst of power and light to redeem
the collapsing air, a little bang of our own creation.
Those afternoons we practiced our kind of alchemy
in your basement, mixing powders and fluids
into horrid smells and eerie colors.Once a pale yellow
foam kept foaming and foaming, threatening to chase
us from the basement and overfoam the world.
Who needed instructions for guided experiments?
Anything worked, and how much better to create
our own concoctions from scratch, to discover
what strange new things were waiting to be made.
Lost in play and laughter, we lost our plan
and for a while found the right ingredients
to transmute the dark that was multiplying
even then in your bones and veins.

Blood Ties

It was not unusual for my cat
to sleep all night beneath my bedcovers,
in the warm, tented space
between my eleven-year old legs.
But that night her belly was full
and sagging, and even now I can't believe
I slept through the entire thing,
waking before everyone else to find
the insides of my sheets and thighs sticky
with dark blood and six tiny sightless
squirming bodies feeding down there
in that secret place,
as if born out of me—
forever implicated,
one of the family.

What Goes Around

In junior high we grew old enough
to practice terror, and one boy learned
my name to become my nightmare.
His shadow waited down every hallway,
in every doorway, followed me home
and hid deep inside my bony body
confused with sex and painful longing.
He taught me the sharp hardness
of words and fists and the metal doors
of lockers against my cornered back,
until I fell through one door
into a country all sharp and small.

Then a smaller boy said something
and I turned and threw him
against a metal door, held him there
hard, trying to make him take my terror.

Some Mornings

When they came for you, I was sleeping.
That day was born to strange voices and feet
scuffing the stairwell outside my bedroom.
"Don't let him in here," you told my mother
in the days before. "I don't want him to see me."
Knowing without knowing, I pulled my blanket
over my head and stilled my breath, pretending
I wasn't there to witness the stopping
of your broken, laughing heart.

There was a morning you always remembered,
that time I ran a good hundred yards over snow and ice
in pajamas and bare feet just to wave goodbye.
I found you in the passenger's seat of our frozen car,
my father at the wheel, your face laughing surprise
through a hole scraped free of frost, about to pull away,
already disappearing into the distance of your life,
leaving me stranded there in my cold.

So I had to see what I could that other morning
from my bedroom window at the last: your form
draped in blue and strapped in black, carried
between two uniformed men, slid into the back
of the shiny white ambulance, the door
closed, pulling away with no siren wailing,
no lights flashing, just disappearing
forever at the end of the driveway.

There was a game I'd play
some mornings after that,
without thought or memory,
when I'd wake into breaking light.

I'd pull my blanket over my head
and lie still in the muffled dark,
and pretend I was riding
in an ambulance somewhere,
dying, dying, or already dead—
as if I might follow again
and find where you had gone.

Ambition

I'm ambitious
to be a good friend,
one whose listening opens
an inner gate
to let you gallop free
in the wild.

I'm ambitious
to be here, to hear
that caw that comes
from the far trees
and draws the looking out.

I'm ambitious
to honor the strangeness
of crystal diatoms and coral reefs,
earwigs and acidophilus;
to praise the fiery-throated fruiteater
and the wall-eyed barracuda
that looked me in the eye when I
was eight years old
and let me swim on
into my life.

I'm ambitious
to disappear
through my eyes
into an iris or a raven,
to gaze into sky and ocean
until my mind turns
into sky and ocean,
into nothing and all;

to enter the world
through each particular
and wake into this skin,
to touch and become
what lives to die
and what lives on.

*In the emerging theory of living systems the process
of life is identified with cognition, the process of knowing.
The interactions of a living organism—plant, animal, or human—
with its environment are cognitive, or mental interactions.
Mind is immanent in matter at all levels of life.*
—Fritjof Capra, The Web of Life

Message to Descartes

an eye looks out from the middle
of the whole, where all is
middle: no outside, no final
edge in this web of sky leaf ant skin
virus dirt badger mind iris wind

mind in a cottonwood creating itself
in each moment—a transubstantiation
of earth air water seed light mind
in the purple morning-glory that knows
the dark and knows the light through and through
mind in the six brown ants that carry the thread
of a desiccated earthworm across
the hard-packed dirt, past my feet
encountering the gray stone in their path
ant mind in each, each one stopping
to register the presence of obstacle
then changing their path together, grass
mind in the grasses greening the mountain
dandelion mind in a single dandelion
in the yard, in a single cell, in the nucleus
keeping and sending the code, mind
in every living thing everywhere
you look, Rene, everywhere you look.

Unidentified

I didn't appear in this morning's paper
or on the nightly show, and I won't appear
in next year's news either. In my presence
official words move quickly and try
to avoid my eternal stare. I live
somewhere beyond those mountains
or wherever people remember how to breathe
now and then, for a moment or a life.
Children carry my secret treasure
with pieces of candy and lint in their pockets,
then forget where they buried me in the woods.
In my absence people turn away
from themselves and each other
and try to live on a strict diet
of gossip, rumor, and cold sense.
Cast your line out far and I swim in near.
I dream in your bed when you're not there.
I come all the way from before
the beginning—now I'm here.

Kochia

Green stars rise
out of the ground
pale and soft
fine furs so
delicate and yet
so at home
in the cold
rain and wind
and the dark
down under where
rhizomes dream into
matter, taking hold.

*(Kochia: a tenacious weed of the goosefoot family,
common to the western U.S.)*

How the World Dreams Us

Can I love the earwig that startles
out of my dog's dish in the late evening
like some cockroach cousin with his shiny
brown shell, twitching antennae, sharp tail pincers?
Can I praise the feel of those minuscule feet
scrabbling over the skin of my bare foot
when he falls and makes his escape?
And how about the watersnake slowly swallowing
the dead trout four times its size, pulling it headfirst
down the distending core of its tapered black length?
And the bottleflies and yellowjackets stirring the air
around snake and fish, wanting in on the feast?
Can I love *these*? Can I honor the hawk
that claims my cat in the night?

If I say no, will I die
inside my fear-cocoon?
If I say yes, will I open
into what I fear? Will I be
claimed by the living world, become
a brother to shells, pincers, scales, wings
and what moves within?

We are the life that wants to live
in the midst of other life that wants to live.
                                        —Albert Einstein

After the Aquarium

After the stingrays rising,
                    gliding
and diving
                    through green-blue
on bird wings,
and the loose columns
of plate-faced lookdowns
waving
          like curtains
touched
          by wind;
after the ominous sharks,
the sun-bright tiger-fish,
the ghost crabs, the unseen
          barracuda,
and the strong-jawed morays
silently growling from their holes
in sunken stone, long lost
cousins of snake and men;
after holding our faces to walls
                    of glass
                    to fill
                    our eyes
with that swarm
              of color and form
and the myriad eyes
looking back,

we drive home up the mountain
toward schools of flat-bottomed clouds
swimming the blue above
the Sangre de Cristos,
while a man and a boy
            in the middle
            of the desert,
            in the middle
            of a green field,
make a red triangle
                weave
            and dive
through the luminous depths
of this afternoon.

The House of Today

You startle into wakefulness, your glance
flying around the room, searching for a way
in through the light lifting the ceiling
or the shadows dissolving the walls
or the patterns holding the curtains
and the rails and bars of your crib.
Where? Where?
The only answer I can give
is to softly, softly speak your name,
calling you into the immense house of today.

For Argos MacCallum

To an Actor

I saw you the day they shot John Lennon
and years later in 6th century India, and once
as yourself, sitting in the unfocused sun
as you talked with a friend and watched
the daily parade along the Paseo.
Madman and sage, murderer, prince
and bloke—a thousand names
and one face, changing features
to inhabit each human instance,
our possibilities made palpable,
our ghosts embodied.

Two thousand miles and a life
off Broadway, before a small
gathering of darkened faces,
you enter the light and turn
those simple, worn boards
into ground of shared being,
anyplace and everyplace,
the only place that matters.

Even now if I close my eyes,
the curtain rises and I see
your image, shifting shape,
take the waiting stage.

First Identity

What am I
without the earth,
without the light,
without the rain?

I wake to eat grain
fed by the falling light
and meat fed with the grain
that rises out of the ground
fed by the falling light
and returning rain.
I breathe the breath of trees
that breathe the breath of me,
wear fiber spun from seed and sun,
drink milk and wine that pour
from the first rain, falling
and rising to fall and rise
in other forms and names.

I am the earth,
I am the light,
I am the rain.

II

A Far Country

En Route

Radio static,
cows and clouds,
curve of space.
The dark line
of the horizon
is a shelf
holding the sky.
All day we drive
toward that place
as if toward
some reckoning
we never quite reach.

What is it
within us that dreams
into distance?

Night
in a temporary bed
and your touch
troubles the water
of a landlocked sea.
Current conducts, pulse
of a secret code,
a wordless message
from the border.

First Sky

Some days you don't need a second sky—
the one outside is what you have
to learn. However you step your step is off, as if
someone moved the ground around while
you were off visiting the vanished islands
of your sleep, or clinging to the beaten raft
of your sleeplessness. Then it's a matter of
remembering your wife's name when
you say her name, remembering how to
walk when you walk, how to be
your pilgrim self. Be glad then
for what the ordinary light or a random
crow or the ice sealing the lake
can teach you. Remember where
you and your life agreed to meet.
Walk out on the wide day toward
that place, listening hard with your feet.

Local

In that empty field at the edge
of the neighborhood, where stray dogs run,
cans rust, ants thrive, and sometimes
a drunk man sleeps in the sun behind the fence,
tall grasses whisper and rustle up to your ear.
You walk by and think you hear voices
telling their old stories, mouths moving
in swirls of grass and wind, scattering
scraps of sense in the indifferent afternoon.
What do those voices have to do with you?
And why those stories? You hear
they're going to build houses here soon,
filling this emptiness for once and all.
The grasses will find another home, but
what about those voices?
Now and then in vacant moments you think
you hear someone asking: Where do *you* live?

The Tilelayer

arrives too early,
plays bad seventies radio music too loud,
smokes weed but says Jesus saved him
from smack and burglary,
and tries to save recalcitrant me
over coffee and shredded wheat.

Fifty-six, he says, proud
of veined arms and young man's waist,
hands hard as claws.
You're kidding, I say, though
his brown eyes are old
as light and pain.

When I return that evening
he's already gone
and the bathroom floor has become
a shimmering pattern,
cobalt and bone white,
flawed and fine,
the silent echo
of a single word
in the heart of hard matter.

Next Door

It takes all you know and feel
   and a world more
      to see a human being.

Take anybody—that body
   just passing by—
      that singular star

at the center of space,
   that transient
      source of light, unique

home of final darkness.
   Try to imagine
      a whole other life,

pole to pole,
   and its burning core—
      not as your own, familiar

yet too close to see,
   but the way you might look
      if you came to a window

at night and noticed the glow
   of a neighboring window,
      a flicker of shadow,

a partial shape,
   and paused a moment or two
      before closing the blinds,

your seeing quickened
   by the invisible.

The Latest News

I might have stayed inside the fence
of my thought, but then those juncos
brushed the surface of my sight—quick
scattering through hallways of pine
calling me out into that farther, closer world
where the air breathes now now.

Though mind gropes after the memory
and memory gropes after the fact
to catch and hold each wing's quick flame,
nothing prepares for the coming—juncos
into pines—and all space opens wide.

Cat Carcass

The crows and maggots have long since
left it to this peace, worked by turns
of sun and rain and sun
till it's just the flattened shape
of cat, desiccated hide and chocolate fur
hung on a frame of bone.
Around its neck it still carries
the obscured language of belonging,
but each day the fur bleaches
to become more and more
the color of the sand,
and each day the wind sifts
more sand into the coat.
It lies halfway between
road and river, as if it crawled
from a sudden crushing wheel
toward this sweet murmuring to die.
Somewhere another voice
has stopped calling.

Swish

Late morning basketball
hoop and net abandoned
by kids back in class.
The wind plays alone.

In a Fog

The world has gone away.
Only the muffled sighs
of the interstate and the phantom
clatter of trains passing through
on their way somewhere definite.
Who could guess us here
within this edgeless cloud?
What is close comes closer
and is all we have,
though even the house next door
has forgotten its address
and wandered into dream.
When the sky finally comes back
to find us, we too may be gone.

This Fire

Dying quietly
at my desk,
afternoon, in the middle
of some empty task,
I look up and out
into a cottonwood: a screen
of conspiring green,
and within: a hidden
galaxy
of layered leaves
dreaming the light,
flashing and flickering
through deep space between.

I could stare into this fire
until my eyes fuse
with the beckoning flames.

Tracking

Frozen here in the red mud for this time being,
these tracks speak the moment of our passing:
shoe and horseshoe, paws of dog and coyote,
scratches of squirrel and bird, maybe others
obscured in the general muddle, gone ahead
of us down into that great silence where all
the stories begin. We ourselves have vanished
into lives we never expected to know, distances
that reached out of our dreaming, or that came
to meet us out of the dark. If you try to follow, know
that sooner or later the trail will grow cold, our tracks
dissolving into the ordinary dust, and you'll be left
in some far place with only one, intermittent star
that recalls the way you've come. But now, look down:
already your marks are added to our melting names.

Santa Fe River, West of Saint Francis

Below the highway's oscillating drone,
these red-brown walls worked by time.
Long roots, coarse as rope or fine
as vein, reach down
the etched and layered faces
after the memory of singing water.
Here lost things gather
in a public oblivion
among beer cans, broken glass
and fading fast food wrappers.
A bright yellow tennis ball
like a miniature sun
held motionless in a slab of ice.
A maimed kite bleeding red
into the wide evening light.
A wood-handled hacksaw
still whole, sinking into sand
beneath the steady trickle.
A pair of black gloves resting
on a dry brown stone.

Somewhere a man opens
an old box, and water
restores his sight.

What have I left behind
that I meant to return for?

A Boy Fishing

Too late to tell you now,
I tell this anyway,
for my own hearing.
How I'd wake to your voice
in the darkness, your shape
at the door, the hallway bright behind you.
How I'd rise with your two boys
from my cot between their beds
to cold cereal, toast, and apple butter,
then fall back to sleep in the backseat
of the only car on the road,
as you pushed the headlights
through the tunnel of night
toward the water waiting
at morning's distant edge.
And there in the cool gray quiet
walking through tall wet grasses
to where the mist was rising
off the liquid stillness,
the roof of the lake
falling away with the light
and the beginnings of birds.
How, years before the stroke
that took your speech and motion,
years before your quiet death,
you showed me the way
to cast my line far out
where my bait would fall into the depths
of peace that still open in me,
even now, as I fish with these words.
How, for a little while,

I could forget the vast absence
of my own father,
and just be a boy
in that waking world
with you and your boys,
a boy fishing.

Morning

An arm of sunlight stretches
across the carpet to rest
its warm weight on my chest.
The dog and the cat asleep
on the couch, the blending
notes of nearby birds.
Somewhere a clock
counts for no one.

Long Distance

You may not know the meaning
of your own voice
heard across this distance,
how your laughter unleashes
my laughter, saying
come out and play
after long silent years,
we grow old only once,
a little more each day.

You may not know how your voice
strikes sparks, like two rocks
knocked together, igniting
sleeping wood, cloth, air.

You may not know how my inner ear
follows your trail of words,
tracing the phosphorescent path
in the wake of a boat at night
far out to sea, where the dark
water deepens into knowing.

You may not know that your words
are live current crackling
over counted, countless miles of line
to light a solitary room.

I'm telling you now.

In the Check-out Line

Her face is bruised and clawed,
three red stripes still raw
down the side of her neck.
Her eyes are wild animals
that keep hidden from sight,
her movements quick with fear,
as if any moment that familiar shadow
might come from anywhere,
again, even here.
She rings up our soap and envelopes,
our vitamins and dog food,
beer and medicine, her pain
all that's left uncounted.
One-by-one she tells us
to have a nice day.
I think of something to say,
but I say nothing.
None of us says anything.
The silence is a desert
we do not cross.

History of the Blues

Somebody did somebody wrong.

A Gift

We were talking high abstraction,
saving or dooming the world as we walked
evening streets of the city
after the graduate seminar.
There were probably people passing,
their faces and backs concealing
and revealing the lives within,
but I wouldn't have noticed.
There must have been trees
here and there, and the various buildings
in that part of town. I wasn't there
or anywhere, and knew no way back.

Then: "*Look* at this light," you said
in the middle of our distant words,
and glancing up where you gestured
with your hand, I saw the ceiling
of the city loved by the last of the sun.
I remembered the thick, slow heat,
the coming summer, the evening pouring
us all down into the great ocean of night.
Something stirred and came within touch.

I kept that light.

A Meaning of Wildflowers

I go back to find the wildflowers
flowering again, in the same place
beside the pouring stream: bluebells
and purple mountain aster, yellow
and white yarrow, crimson paintbrush,
orange-crowned columbine, others
I can't place, myself the one displaced.
Does it matter that I can't explain
the deep gladness that rises
to meet this bounty rising
from the tangled darkness?
Here words seem too forgetful
of silence and the kind of sense
a flower or a stream might speak.
Meanwhile these colors and forms
pour through parched valleys
to light the hidden seeds
and wake a sleeping ocean.

A Far Country

From somewhere in sleep I wake
to a tapping soft and constant as rain
on the window, but not.
My dog whines and yelps
in the darkness the way she does
when chasing rabbit and deer
deep into desert and forest
where I can't see
and her name can't follow,
leaving me to worry and wonder if
someday, caught up in the wild
hunt, she might not make it back
to her canned food and comfort
of sleep beneath the bedside table.

More tapping like unknown code
and then I know it's her
nails clicking against the wall,
legs twitching in pursuit
or flight, a faint echo
from a far country.
I start to call her name,
then close my eyes instead.

The Transient River

Today the sunlight arrives
like a benediction, and I'm here
to receive this love, I'm not afraid
of this wild happiness, I'm willing
to be born into the opening air
like the birds leaving the baring branches.
Today I don't hurry the hands of the clock
but walk into the space between.
Today the river doesn't hurry, slowly
braiding itself down its golden back,
its sandy bed rearranged from yesterday
and the day before and the day before: the sift
and drift of water, silt and wearing stone, particles
and molecules continually shifting, being
made and making, forming and unforming,
a kaleidoscope turning unseen, seen, unseen.
Today I walk so long in the light, the sun
gets in my eyes and flows in my veins
and I see that nothingness is nothing
but the door through which all being
comes and goes and comes again.
Today I find this transient river
come again from somewhere near
and all I have loved,
all I love,
all love
flowing
here.

How to Change

A bear looms on the path ahead,
wavering in the light that wavers
when the wind rearranges the trees.
Then bear becomes a clump of grass
and dirt atop an abandoned fencepost
dissolving into the ground, into the air.
An old friend calls unexpectedly
to tell the news of a different place.
You wake in the dark in another life.
Lilacs sing, heat blooms, crickets shine
and what can you do, can you do
but stand where you are, wherever, wherever
and let the light flow through.

Home
in the
Dark

Arrival

Then we lowered from the blue roof
into white, that first whiteness
flickering with quick curtains of light,
but then, deeper, only white
and more white, and more, a whiteness
that kept rising and rising
out of some bottomless nowhere.
                                    We kept on
talking as if that white were nothing,
not nothing.
                    We touched the details—
work and families, where we were going—
as if to make the world real again
against the ghostliness glancing in windows
still white between words, though once
I saw some gray shape that vanished
back out of sight. By then I knew
I was the ghost that haunted
that whiteness, remembering
who I had been, as if already
forgetting, already,
already . . .

Walking the Silence

Water striders walk over leaves
that whisper underwater colors
river talks around rocks
otter glides through a roof
of sky, inside out: liquid news

what the red-winged blackbird says
what the red-winged blackbird says

murmur of tattered cattails
something moving within
seed fluff climbing up
a stairway of wind

hum of fallow wheat fields
hum of the full moon
hum of father to frightened son
in the deep of the dark

rain falling like sleep
rain falling like sleep

footsteps over frosted grass
ten thousand ways back.

Pendleton Reverie Before Bed

In the clear distance of night
a truck's lights slide along the interstate
toward the Blue Mountains,
a presence hidden
in the blackness beyond.
Then I'm along for the ride—
taking the rise up Cabbage Hill,
farmland, desert, and great river falling
away behind; thirty-seven miles to La Grande
through dense tamarack and pine,
all the sleeping, creeping wild.

The First Terror

In the evening in an empty arroyo
outside of town, a man in a white dress
slowly walks to where he sleeps alone
every night, under a retreating sky
and stars distant as lost memory, among
the silent cedar, the dust and the stones.
When he begins to scream at the voices
screaming in his head, the sound breaks
the still surface of dusk, reverberating
through ancient foothills to find
the inner ear of a distant stranger,
calling up fear, sudden and fresh.

He stops to listen, hand holding a cup
or touching a newspaper, and tries to place
that sound: somebody being attacked
by wild animals, or somebody
attacking somebody else.
But then he remembers
the man in the white dress
descending alone into night,
and he knows his own terror
comes from a place old and deep,
a child's bed falling through the dark,
the weight of nothing, falling.
He knows what night can do.

A Place I Go

Ends of some days I climb up
into the hills above town
so I can see what's down here
and remember where I am.
There's a juniper bush up there
that once spoke to Moses,
its needles still burning with the light
that says all creation's aflame.
Up there the wind won't call you
by your given name, but if you listen long
enough it will tell you who you are.
Blend in with what surrounds you—this grass
and sky, these ants, those mountains—
and the birds will treat you like family,
singing your prodigal self home.
You can sit there in the peace
that contains even your deepest terror,
and watch this part of the planet
spin away from the last of the sun,
and go on being.

Advice to Myself

Be skeptical of cynicism,
especially the chronic kind,
that paralysis of soul.
You know less than you think
and much more, as body
sometimes teaches mind
and part teaches whole.
So remember the elephant's trunk
when holding its tail in your hand.
When standing under,
try to understand.

The Old Woman and the Gray Cat

When the gray cat with matted fur arrives at the
glass door, surfacing again out of winter's wide maw,
the old woman with bad teeth stops flipping burgers
long enough to bring two pieces of half-stale bacon.
She does not lecture the cat on politics or theology
or the trouble with stray cats in today's world. "There
you are," she says, placing the pieces of bacon on
the cold cement, then returns to her work.

The gray cat with matted fur eats every crumb,
then wanders off into the weeds around the side of
the building, disappearing into the gray beyond the
railroad tracks.

Home in the Dark

One evening walking alone
an absent-minded path that kept climbing
foothills into coming night,
I suddenly saw I'd gone too far
to beat the darkness home.
(Was that what I'd wanted all along?)
I turned and started back
the way I'd come, different now
in darkness and direction,
the difference all my own,
and as I went I witnessed
night's gradual saturation—
how it claimed the sky and the trees,
the stones, the path, and me.
It took me in as if I belonged
with all the rest, and always had.
My fear came out to chase me back,
but I turned and looked
into his fearful eyes, for once
too much at home to fight.
We took each other in, and walked together
as one descending with the dark,
with distant coyotes singing the night
and the wind singing through needle and bark,
as shapes shed their daylight
names to become their singular selves
slowly dissolving into one, as one
descending with the dark
into a peace deep as death,
some bottomless love
filled with the presence
of every hidden color.

Current

Near sleep, lightning
slices the dark space
behind my eyelids
mountains shudder, the air
tears open and I wake
into this river flowing
everywhere, a passenger
again, alive, at home
in the going.

On Leaving My Colleagues at the Nursery

Goodbye now. I'll remember you
by your dreams: that nightmare
about the rose bush you moved all night
from there to there to there.
The idea of going back to school
or leaving to find better work
in San Diego or Mexico, someplace.
The fish that waited and waited
for your rusting hook.
The longing for something else,
something else, something else
you could not say.

It was not the unloading
of countless black buckets
to count, cart, tag, and display,
not the demeaning arguments
of the disgruntled wealthy,
not the minuscule wages that evaporated
as quickly as the water we sprayed
on golden rain trees and butterfly bushes
withering in the mid-summer desert sun.
(Those plants became our kin,
brothers and sisters,
children from a different branch
of the same garden.)

I am left with your work-wracked bodies,
the smell of your sweat, your scarred hands,
breaking backs and stunned eyes,
the sounds of your voices weaving
through leaves of cottonwood and willow,

your anger, jokes, and revelations—
the deaths of children, addictions,
the virus that lurked in the blood—
and your silences, your silences.

I see you at the end of the day
filing out of the common cage
into the space that remains before sleep.
I speak you in what words I'm able.
I keep you in my silence.

Spirit of the north, of the earth,
of nighttime and winter:
Be with us in the darkness,
in the time of gestation.

—Native American prayer

In the Dark

Now the flame goes down
to gather again in the roots.
Now the bear withdraws
with the birds and the light.
Now time falls slowly, slowly
as the snow, as the embryo
blossoms in its blind ocean,
while we tend a small fire
and wait, grieve, dream, sleep
through beginnings already
forming in the dark,
in the time of gestation.

A Legacy

I had counted up your sins,
numbered your absences
and intimate errors:
what I needed
and you didn't give,
what I didn't
and you did.

I wanted human sounds,
close words to tame the dark,
but you gave me silence
and the voices of rivers—
Potomac and Colorado,
Salmon and San Juan—
fluid sounds that conjured
songs from my sleep
and woke me to first singing,
the shaping of notes
only for myself
and the sympathetic trees.

I wanted eyes that opened
a place for me in the opening world,
but you looked away
into landforms and vistas
where I wandered after
your vision, dreaming
my way into my own,
learning my solitude
and the kinship of lizards
and coral, squirrels and reeds.

Then the alligators spoke
from their ocean of grass
and I understood
how the feral light,
the singing green,
the starred and creatured dark
had always blossomed
for my ears and eyes.

I knew what I would keep.

Letter of Apology to the Nonliving

Dear dirt, stars, rain, wood, air
breathed in, blood-carried to my heart:
Dear central sun and magma core,
great plates, mountains and oceans
that open beyond map and mind:
Dear forgotten skeletons disintegrating
in fields, forests, graveyards, deserts,
calcium and carbon ghosts
of ancestors, cousins, friends:
Dear fire, fiber, rock, space, wind,
hydrogen, sulfur, nitrogen:
Please accept my profuse apologies
for how deeply I live in sleep.
As if you were mere background—
mere resource, scenery, furniture, stage.
As if I could dream myself into being
without your conspiring.
As if I did not live
every moment
in your visible and invisible arms.

The Time of Great Blue Heron

Two great blue heron keep this river.
Now and then they find us, alone
or together, flowing overhead
on long, deep beats of wing,
or fishing the shallows with slow steps
on hinged stilts, then
meteor stabs of beak;
and sometimes, if we're lucky
and have nowhere to be,
they emerge from night-shadowed reeds
on reed-legs,
moving through scattered patches
of black water
shimmering with moon.

The clock resumes and the days forget
river, sky, moon, wings, and eyes.

Then the great blue heron come again.

Crossing Space

on West Texas 84,
you're pulled by pure distance,
mile after mile after mile
of unbroken plain,
the miles becoming something else
until the mind finally
uncoils and releases
into its own
rhythm of going.
Oil derricks appear
like a quiet invasion
of alien creatures come
to feed off the ground
where scraps of cotton
hold on after harvest,
scattered shreds of light
in a galaxy of brown.
Now and then a house
suddenly arrives
at the roadside,
at the edge
of your in between,
a place someone soon
will depart in sleep
beneath the reach
of other headlights.
Faces sometimes
turn to look
at the very moment
you shoot past.
Light passing between stars.

The Trees are Speaking

The trees are speaking
to my four-month old daughter.
She lies on a blanket, looking up
into feathery locust leaves,
kicking and waving in wild pleasure,
talking back in her improvised language
of squeals, screeches and moans,
then suddenly growing quiet
and still as if listening to the voice
of some great mystery
when the wind breathes and the leaves
shudder and murmur their utter nonsense.
In the news old hatreds
renew themselves in word and blood,
while a strange fire consumes the land.
All day I mourn tomorrow.
We fall asleep beneath a thin roof,
under dark branches and leaves
that tremble with the stars.
The trees are speaking.

Gathering Stones

I'm distracted by stones. You should be
doing something worthwhile, a voice says,
instead of this random gathering of rocks for
no clear purpose. Yet I keep to my stones.
Looking always to the horizon, after
apparitions of blind desire, I would miss
the shimmer of mica, the little homecomings
of icy quartz and chameleon granite, the way
pale green lichen spots a massive gray boulder
to make a great whale stranded on an ocean floor
whose ocean lifted long ago to a burning sky,
receding into time and wherever water goes.
Smaller stones I pick up in my hands, each one
singular in its color or shape, texture or weight,
all offspring of first matter, the plain and luminous
debris of that beginning whose tendrils of sound
still spiral into ever-deepening space.
There's something the stones mean
to tell me, I like to think. At least
it feels that way, the stones feel that way
to my fingers and palms. So I put one or two
in my pocket and take them home, until now
a diverse family crowds the hallway table.
Sometimes when I take them up again
in my forgetful hands, there's something in them
that calms beyond all fear and longing.

Then each stone fills my hand's space
like an answer. Maybe it's what they teach
of gravity—not to be afraid of the weight
of these bones, this nervous matter,
but to settle into the wholeness
the way a slow rain falls and falls
all day and night, filling the earth,
the dreaming dust of stones.

Printed in the United States
741500005B

9 780865 343559